Kirigami

Kirigami

Fold and cut to create beautiful paper art

Monika Cilmi

ARCTURUS

ARCTURUS

This edition published in 2018 by Arcturus Publishing Limited
26/27 Bickels Yard, 151–153 Bermondsey Street,
London SE1 3HA

Copyright © Arcturus Holdings Limited

ISBN: 978-1-78428-766-5
AD005631US

Printed in China

Contents

Introduction

The word "kirigami" comes from the Japanese "kiru" (to cut) and "kami" (paper). Paper-cutting in Japan dates from the 4th century AD, soon after the invention of paper in China. Kirigami came to be considered a serious art form in Asian culture from the 17th century onward. In Japan and China, kirigami designs were used to represent "wealth, perfection, grace, elegance, and the relationship with nature and the universe."

Today, kirigami art is used for greetings cards, gift wrapping, home decoration projects, wall art, and scrapbooks. Kirigami is also taught in schools as part of the curriculum, because primary symbolism is very important in Asian culture. Kirigami gives students the opportunity to learn about the importance of Japanese culture while developing visual motor and planning skills.

Materials

Symmetry is very important in kirigami. This is evident from the designs, which tend to be the same on both sides. Kirigami deploys various folds and bases; the three bases used in this book are rectangular, square and triangular. With certain types of kirigami, you can create three-dimensional effects by cutting the design in some areas and not in others.

Rectangular base
This base can be made in various widths and thicknesses, from a single fold to four repeated folds (into eighths).

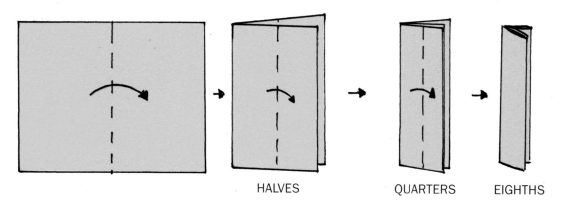

HALVES   QUARTERS   EIGHTHS

Square base

This base consists of a vertical followed by a horizontal fold.

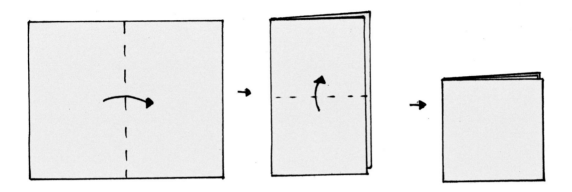

Triangular base

To make the triangular base, fold the paper on the diagonal, then fold the resulting triangle in half.

Measure an angle of 60°, then fold over the points as shown, making sure your shape is symmetrical.

HALVES

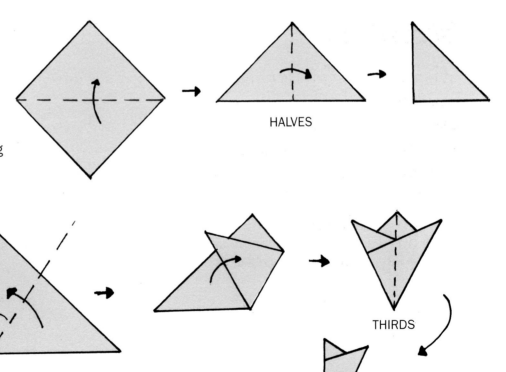

THIRDS

SIXTHS

Introduction

Essential materials and tools for kirigami consist of the following:

- a pencil

- paper and card

- a craft knife

- scissors

- glue stick or double-sided tape

- a cutting mat

- a ruler

- a protractor (for measuring angles)

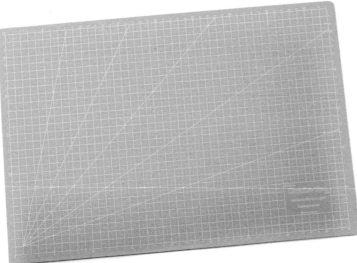

Any type of paper or card is suitable for kirigami, though thinner paper is best for projects that involve lots of folds. You can use scissors to make the cuts, but a craft knife is necessary for thicker card and internal detailed cutting. The knife needs to be sharp, so it's important to use a cutting mat to protect the work space and provide a flat surface on which to do your cutting. A ruler is useful for measuring paper sizes and keeping folds in place. A glue stick or double-sided tape may be necessary for joining various paper structures and completing greetings cards.

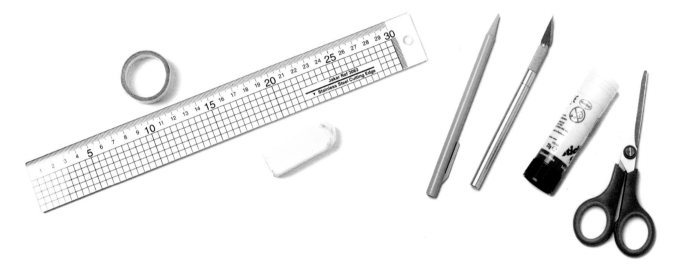

Getting started

Creating kirigami can be confusing at first, so here are some basic steps to help you start your projects:

1. Draw the design

You can draw your design directly onto paper or print it on copy paper and tape the paper to the final card before cutting through both layers at once. Alternatively, print the design on the reverse of your final card and cut it out back to front.

2. Cut along the lines

Once you've created your design, cut it out using a craft knife or scissors.

3. Fold, display, and illuminate

When you have completed all your cuts and made your model, you can use LED lighting to illuminate the different planes of your design and turn it into an eye-catching work of art.

In order to create 3D-style kirigami, you need to be aware that everything works along a principal fold. A basic rule of 3D kirigami is shown in the diagram below, where two perpendicular vertical lines are cut across the principal fold, then the paper is folded horizontally to create a cube.

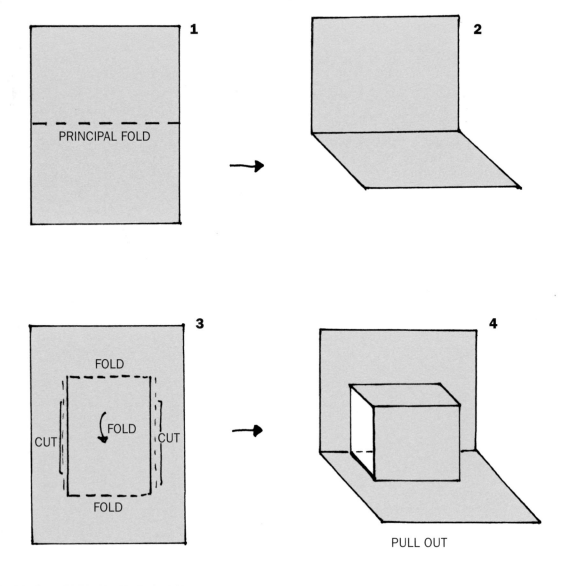

Nature and Animals

This section is inspired by the beauty of nature and features kirigami in the shape of animals, flowers and other natural forms. Some pieces are simple cut-outs while others are 3D projects.

Kissing cats

This simple cut-out design includes a pair of kittens to give added interest. You can make it using colored thin card or heavy paper.

1 Use a 21 x 30 cm (8¼ x 11¾ in) rectangular piece of card for this project.

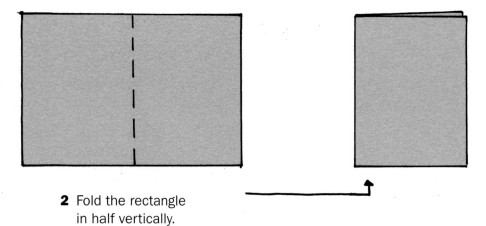

2 Fold the rectangle in half vertically.

3 Using a pencil, draw your cat and kitten, adding the delineation of the animals' forms inside the main design.

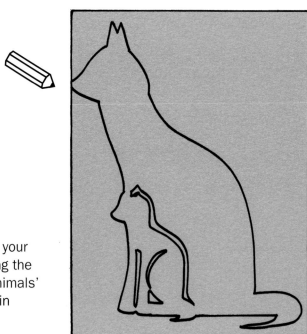

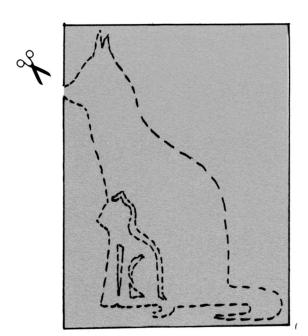

4 Cut along the lines, being careful not to cut where the cat's nose touches the side of the card.

5 Open the card.

You can use your final design as either a card or a decoration.

Trees

This project shows a copse of trees and stands in a zigzag pattern, like a screen. It works best against a contrasting background, with the addition of an LED light to give the effect of sunlight and shadow.

1 Take a piece of medium-thickness rectangular card measuring 21 x 30 cm (8¼ x 11¾ in) and section it into quarters. Draw your design of two tall trees and two shorter trees using a pencil.

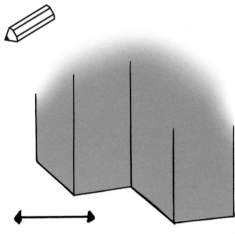

2 Fold the card to make the four creases and then flatten it again.

3 Cut carefully around your design using a craft knife and cutting board.

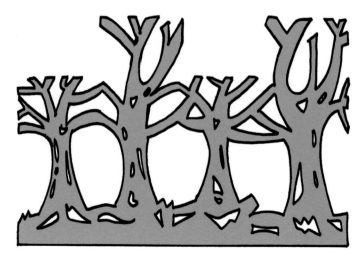

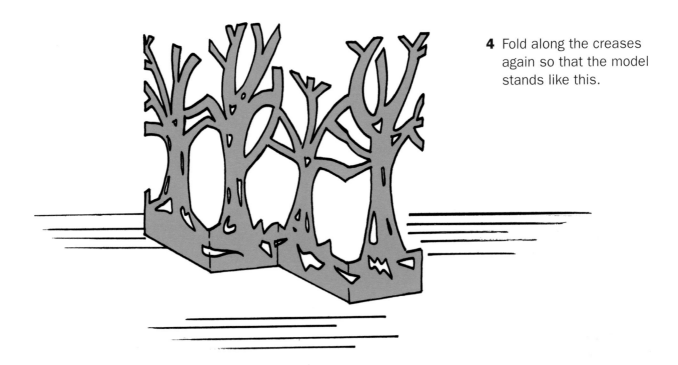

4 Fold along the creases again so that the model stands like this.

Clever LED lighting gives the impression of dappled shade.

Snowflake 1

This project is simple yet effective. You can use white or light blue card instead of paper, but it should not be too thick otherwise it will be difficult to cut when folded. Use a ruler and a craft knife or sharp scissors to get an accurate result.

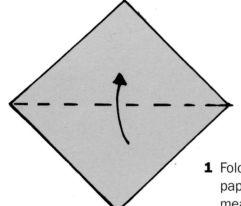

1 Fold your origami paper square measuring 21 x 21 cm (8¼ x 8¼ in) in half along the diagonal.

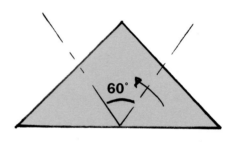

2 Fold in along the dotted lines, as shown, and unfold again.

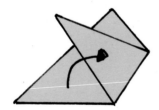

3 Fold over the righthand side.

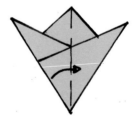

4 Fold the lefthand side on top.

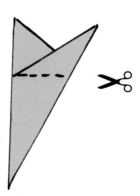

5 Fold the model in half vertically and cut along the dotted line.

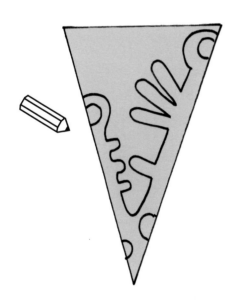

Try adapting the design to produce your own unique snowflake shapes.

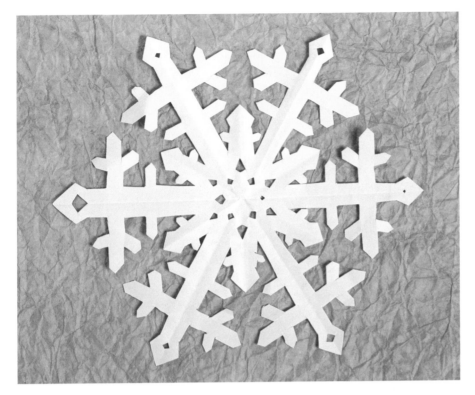

6 Using a ruler, carefully draw the design.

7 Cut around your drawing using scissors or a craft knife.

8 Gently open out your intricate snowflake.

Dolphin

This leaping dolphin is eye-catching and beautiful as a standing 3D design. It looks great against a solid, dark background.

1 Draw your design on a medium-thickness rectangular card measuring 21 x 30 cm (8¼ x 11¾ in), making sure to allow around 1 cm (½ in) at the bottom for the base.

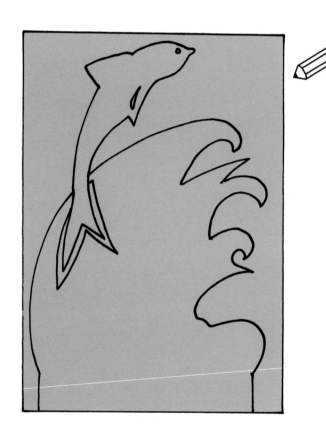

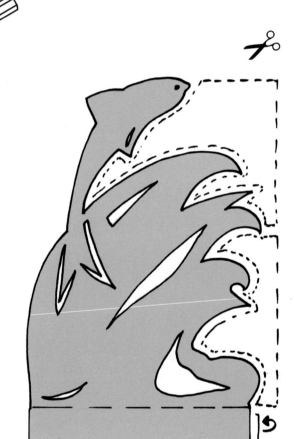

2 Cut around your pencil lines and include some internal cutting, as shown. Don't throw away the pieces of card from your cutting as you will use them as part of the final composition.

3 The first two pieces are left
over from your cutting in step 2.
Now modify the rest of the leftover
card to make the third piece.

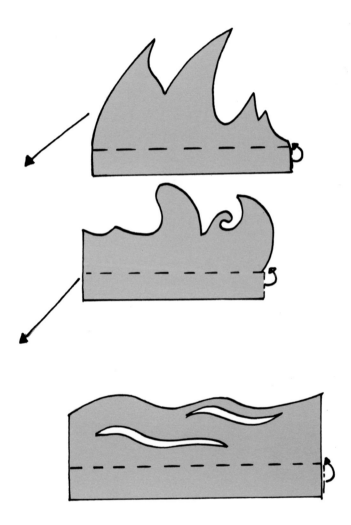

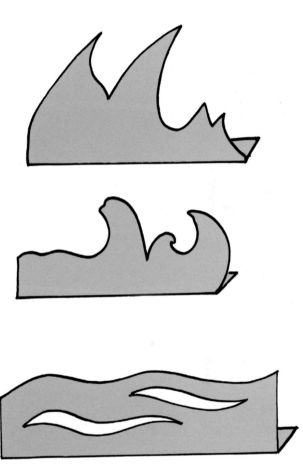

4 Fold the lower flaps under on all three
pieces.

5 Make four cuts, as shown, on a separate piece of card.

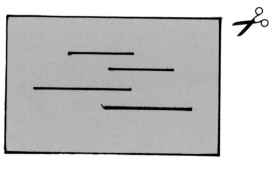

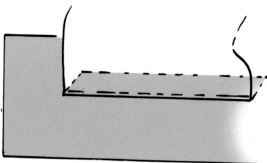

6 Insert the folded bases into the cuts you have just made.

The model looks great with LED lighting, displayed against a dark background.

Wings

This design uses contrasting colors to make the cutting stand out effectively.

1 Using a rectangular sheet of thin card or thick paper measuring 16 x 22 cm (6¼ x 8½ in), draw your design in pencil. You can either use a single piece of card or draw on the righthand side of a folded card, as shown.

2 Cut out the design, being careful to leave the parts attached where shown. Now glue a second sheet of card or paper behind the first; this should be the same size as the first, in a contrasting color.

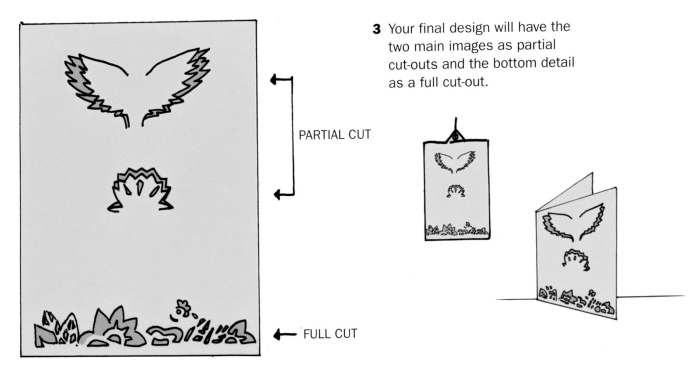

3 Your final design will have the two main images as partial cut-outs and the bottom detail as a full cut-out.

PARTIAL CUT

FULL CUT

You can use the wings as a decorative picture or greetings card.

Flying bird

This effective, dynamic 3D design can either be displayed on the wall as a picture or used as a standing decoration.

This version uses a blue/white color combination to give the effect of clouds and sky.

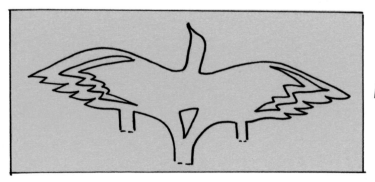

1 Draw your design on a long, rectangular sheet of heavy card measuring 12 x 30 cm (4¾ x 11¾ in). Make sure to include two rectangular tabs on the wings; the tail should also be a long rectangle.

2 Cut out the design, leaving the ends of the three rectangles attached.

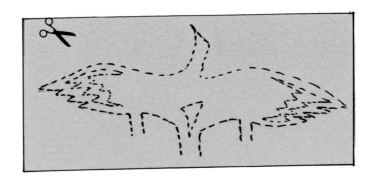

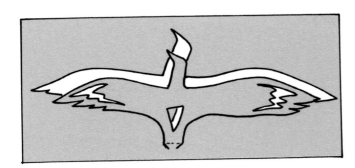

3 Pull out the design, folding the base of the rectangles so that the bird is raised up.

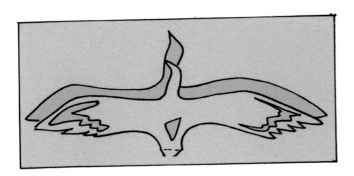

4 Glue a sheet of same-sized card to the back of your design. Use a contrasting color or a blue marbled pattern to resemble clouds (see photo below).

5 You can either hang the flying bird on your wall or create a base with another piece of card to make a standing decoration.

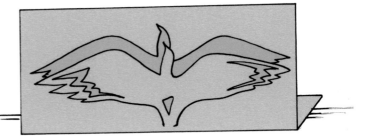

Flower design

This neat, floral graphic design can be used as a simple decoration, framed as a picture or even traced repeatedly as a design for wallpaper.

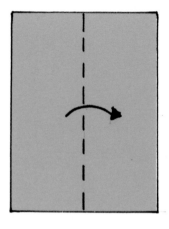

1 Take a sheet of card measuring 21 x 30 cm (8¼ x 11¾ in) and fold it in half.

2 Then fold it in half again.

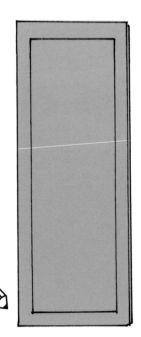

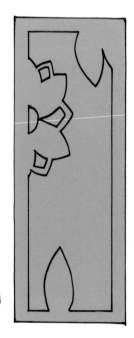

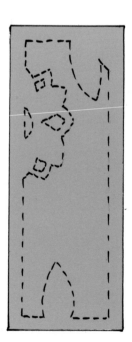

3 Draw a frame of about 1 cm (½ in) in width.

4 Now draw your design, erasing bits of the frame as shown.

5 Cut out the design as indicated by the dotted lines.

6 Open out your card. For an eye-catching effect, glue a sheet of card in a contrasting color to the back.

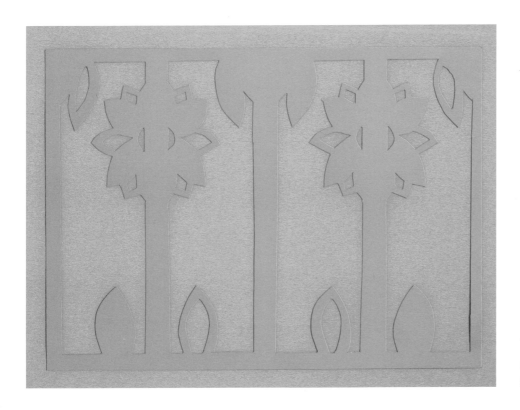

You can fold the model in half to make a greetings card.

Snowflake 2

We all know that no two snowflakes are the same, as this second version demonstrates! This snowflake design is curvier and more detailed than the one on pages 16–17.

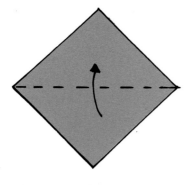

1 This model uses the triangular base folded into sixths. Take a square sheet of paper measuring 21 x 21 cm (8¼ x 8¼ in) and fold it in half.

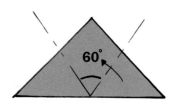

2 Measure a 60° angle from the mid-point and mark it in pencil.

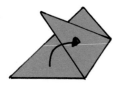

3 Fold in the righthand side along your pencil line.

4 Fold in the lefthand side on top. Now fold the model in half vertically.

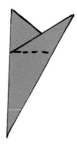

5 Draw a horizontal line across the model and cut along it.

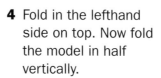

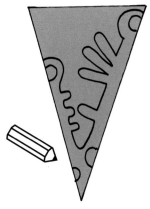

6 Draw the design as shown.

7 Cut out using scissors or a craft knife and cutting mat.

7 Your final piece should look like this.

Make lots of snowflakes in different designs and hang them in your window at Christmas time.

Fish lampshade

This dramatic lampshade features a stylized repeat image
of a Koi carp, made by internal cutting.

1 Using a long, rectangular
sheet of card measuring
17 x 30 cm (6½ x 11¾ in),
create a repeat pattern.

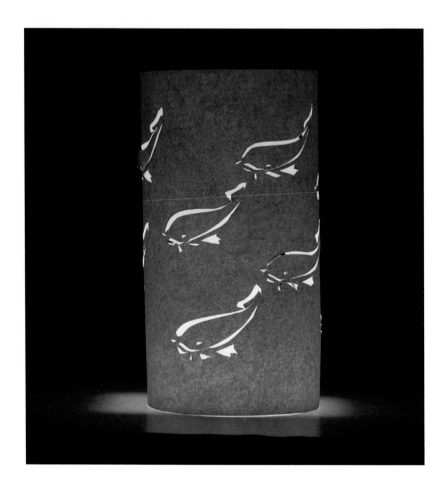

*Made with dark-colored paper,
this model looks very effective
when lit from within.*

2 This detail of the fish shows the lines to be cut.

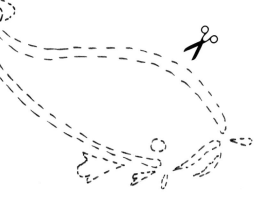

3 Secure the ends of the card by gluing them together. Place the shade over a lamp base of your choice.

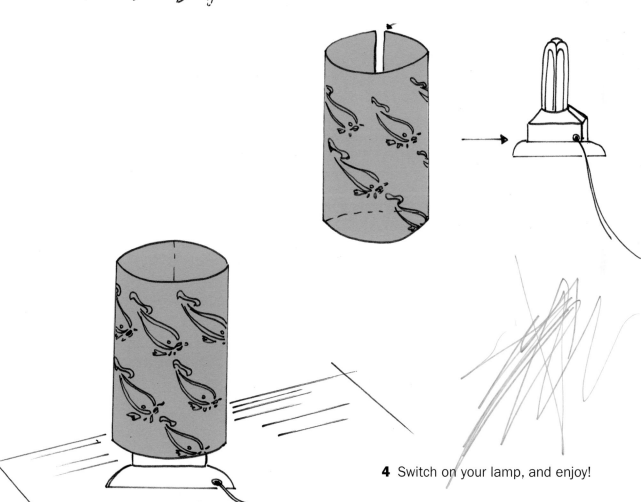

4 Switch on your lamp, and enjoy!

Baby elephant

This 3D model of a baby elephant sitting under a tree makes
a delightful decoration.

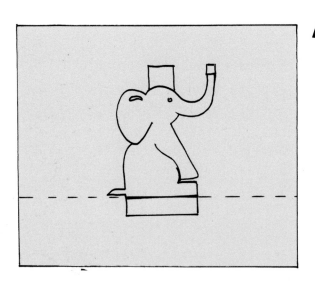

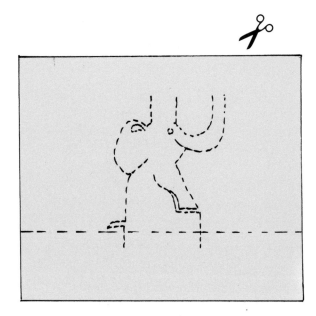

1 Using a rectangular sheet of
card measuring 21 x 30 cm
(8¼ x 11¾ in), draw the elephant
as shown, together with a dotted fold
line for the base. The size after
cutting will be around 21 x 25 cm
(8¼ x 10 in).

2 Cut around the design (but not the
foldline), leaving the head, trunk and
bottom of the elephant attached, as
indicated from the drawing.

3 Fold the card along the base line
and gently pull out the design
while folding the top and bottom
rectangles to keep the shape
in place.

4 Draw the rest of the design and cut it out.

5 Take another sheet of card in a different color, fold it and cut out the shape at the bottom. Glue this card to the back of your model.

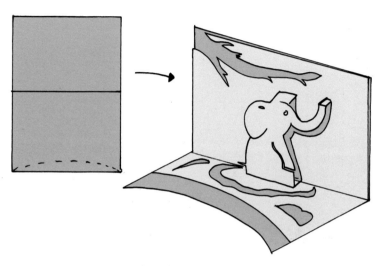

You can also use the finished piece as a greetings card.

Dragonfly

This decorative design, created by partial cutting, mimics a dragonfly resting on a leaf. It looks good as a standing model or hanging on the wall as a picture.

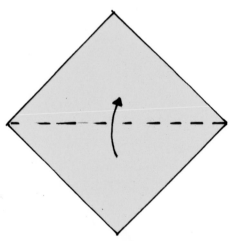

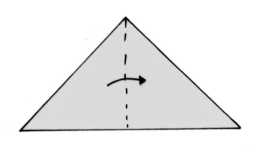

1 Taking a square of paper measuring 21 x 21 cm (8¼ x 8¼ in), fold it up along the diagonal.

2 Fold it in half again.

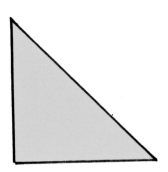

3 This is your triangular base

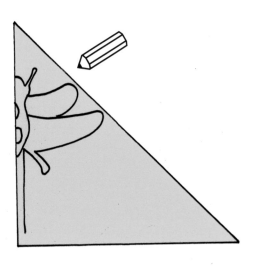

4 Draw your dragonfly design as shown.

5 Cut out along the lines, making sure to stop before you reach the end of the dragonfly's body.

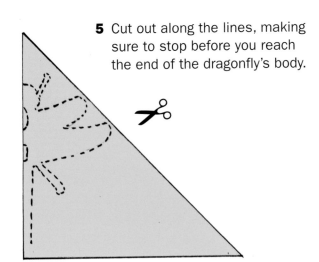

6 Open up the paper and make some freestyle cuts at the two blank corners.

7 Pull up the dragonfly decorations. You can glue another sheet of paper to the back to make a nice contrast.

Lift up some of the foliage at the corners to increase the 3D effect.

Decorative and Structural

The projects in this section are inspired by design and form. They vary from models with spiritual and musical themes to home decorations, some with a Japanese influence.

Table decoration

This design is elegant, with an ethnic theme. It is inspired by a pictographic symbol, meaning "spirit."

1 Take a square sheet of paper measuring 21 x 21 cm (8¼ x 8¼ in) and fold it in half upward on the diagonal.

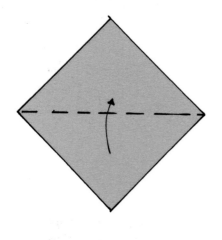

3 Fold in the lefthand side.

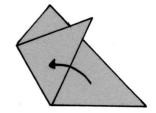

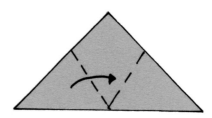

2 Measure a 60° angle from the mid-point.

4 Fold in the righthand side on top.

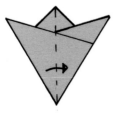

5 Fold in half and cut along the line.

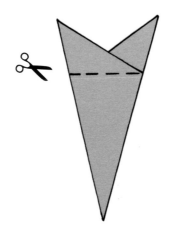

6 Draw the design as shown.

7 Cut out the design with scissors and open up the paper.

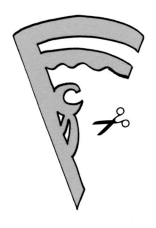

8 Your final piece should look like this.

Use vividly colored paper against a brightly colored tablecloth for an eye-catching effect.

Venetian mask

This project is inspired by the mysterious masks worn by revellers at the Venice Carnival in Italy. I have used the stylized image of a bird for my mask.

1 Take a rectangular piece of card measuring 21 x 30 cm (8¼ x 11¾ in) fold it in half, and draw the design as shown. The tip of the bird's beak should touch the edge of the card.

2 Cut your design out along the lines.

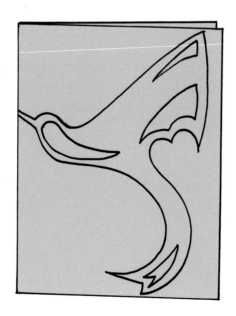

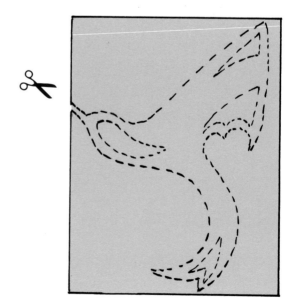

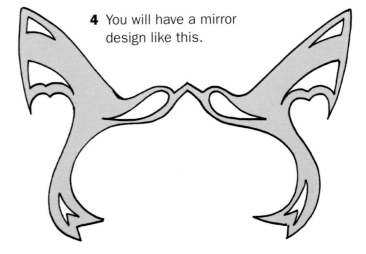

4 You will have a mirror design like this.

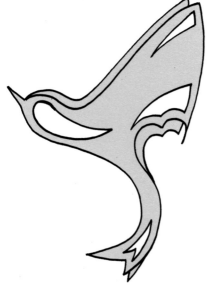

3 Now open out the card.

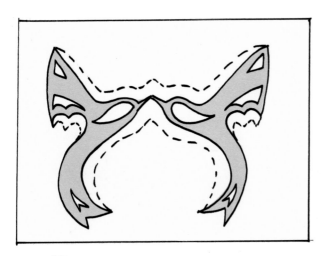

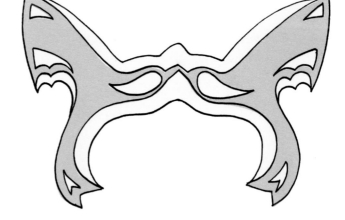

5 Glue your mask onto another piece of card the same size but of a different color and draw round it (shown by the dotted lines). Cut out the mask along these lines.

6 Your finished piece should look like this.

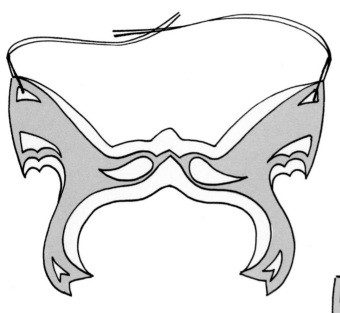

7 Using the cut-out part at the top of the design, attach string or ribbon.

8 Alternatively, you can glue a long stick to the back of the mask.

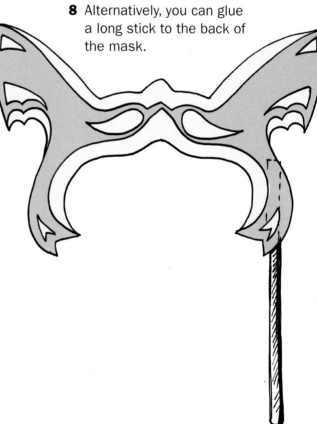

These masks look good on adults, but are also great for children's parties.

Napkin holder

This useful napkin holder is inspired by musical notation, which I have used to create an abstract design

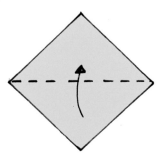

1 Take a square sheet of card measuring 21 x 21 cm (8¼ x 8¼ in), and fold it in half upward on the diagonal.

2 Measure a 60° angle from the mid-point.

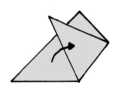

3 Fold in the righthand side.

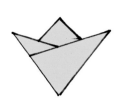

4 Fold the lefthand side on top.

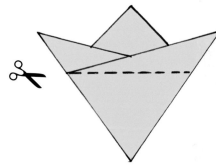

5 Cut along the line.

6 Draw the design as shown and cut round it.

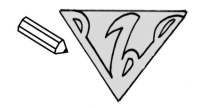

7 Open it out.

8 The finished piece should look like this. Now repeat the process with another sheet of card.

9 Glue each of your finished pieces onto a piece of different-colored card and cut out along the dotted lines.

10 Fold both shapes in half.

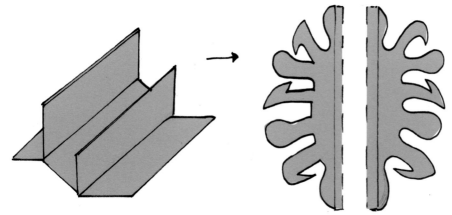

12 This is the structure you want to achieve—your two folded pieces are glued to the base.

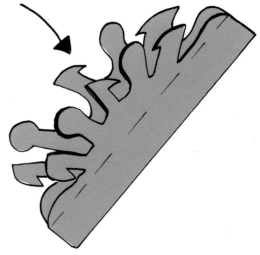

11 Take a piece of card measuring 6 x 21 cm (2½ x 8¼ in) for the base and glue your two designs to it along the fold lines, leaving at least 2.5 cm (1 in) between them.

Your napkin holder is now ready to use.

Japanese pagoda

This model is inspired by Japanese culture. It looks great with a light shining through the 3D design.

1 Draw a pagoda on a sheet of card measuring 21 x 25 cm (8¼ x 10 in), then draw a horizontal pencil fold line across the middle of the card.

2 Cut out the pagoda following the dotted lines shown here.

3 Fold the card along the horizontal line and pull out the shape.

4 Draw a wavy pencil line across the bottom of the card and cut along it. Fold up the card along the line above.

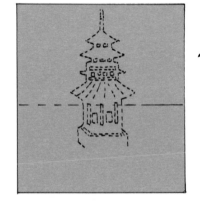

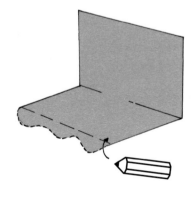

5 With a piece of card in a contrasting color measuring 3 x 21 cm (1¼ x 8¼ in), make irregular cuts along the top and glue it to the inside of the front flap.

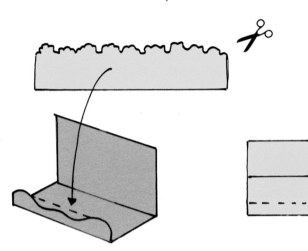

6 Take another piece of card in a contrasting color measuring 21 x 21 cm (8¼ x 8¼ in) and glue it to the back of the model so that it's visible through the cut-out.

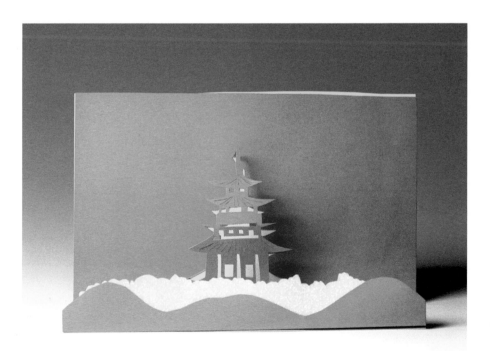

The finished pagoda, seen as part of a stylized landscape.

Geisha screen

Another project inspired by Japanese design, this idea can be adapted to make a full-sized screen to lend privacy to a living-room or bedroom.

1 Take a rectangular piece of card measuring 15 x 26 cm (6 x 10¼ in) and divide it into thirds, marking the divisions in pencil. Then draw the design as shown.

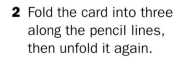

2 Fold the card into three along the pencil lines, then unfold it again.

3 Cut along the lines, making sure you cut both internal and external lines. You may need to use a craft knife and cutting board for this as it's quite intricate.

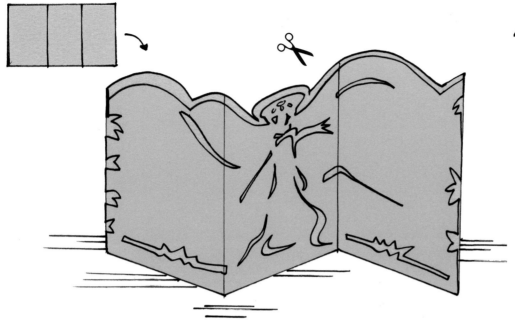

4 Take a piece of different-colored card the same size as the first and glue it to the back of your model. Cut the first card along the top so that the second is visible above the geisha design. Fold the screen and stand it upright.

This abstract design looks great at any size.

Wedding decoration

This piece can be made either as a card or a hanging picture.
The design can also be used on a banner.

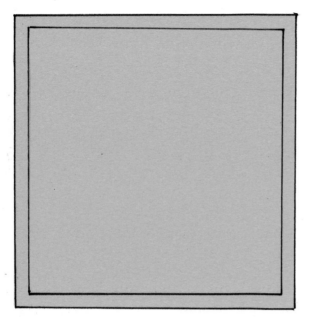

1 Using a sheet of card measuring
16 x 30 cm (6¼ x 11¾ in),
draw a thin frame about
0.5cm (¼ in) wide with a pencil.

2 Draw the design, then erase
parts of the pencil line around
the frame as shown.

3 Cut out the design along the dotted lines.

4 Glue the design to a folded card or banner, or hang it as a picture.

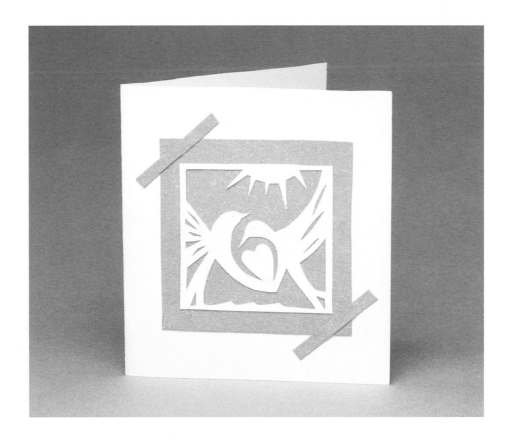

You can modify this design as you see fit.

Hanging decoration

This lovely, simple design works best with patterned or brightly colored paper.

1 You need to use paper for this design—don't use thick card as it will be too difficult to cut. Take a square sheet of paper measuring 14 x 14 cm (5½ x 5½ in) and fold it in half upward on the diagonal.

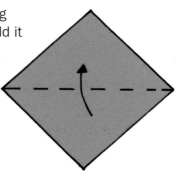

2 Measure a 60° angle from the mid-point.

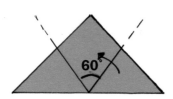

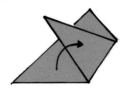

3 Fold in the righthand side.

4 Fold in the lefthand side on top.

5 Cut along the line.

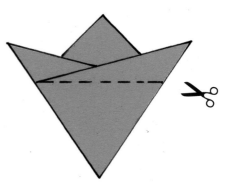

6 Draw the design as shown.

7 Cut round your pencil lines and open out the model.

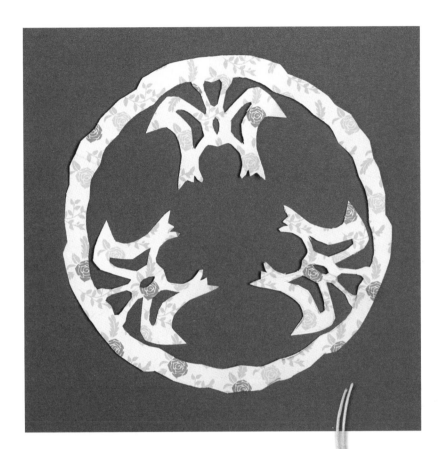

Pale patterned paper makes for a pretty effect.

8 Your final design should look like this. Make a small hole in the border and thread some string through for hanging up.

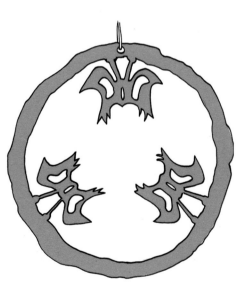

Japanese tea lantern

This design is inspired by the lanterns seen in many Japanese gardens. It follows the basic 3D "L" shape and looks great with some back-lighting.

1 Using a rectangular piece of card measuring 21 x 30 cm (8¼ x 11¾ in), draw the lantern and some grass, leaving space at the top and bottom.

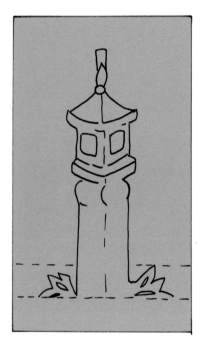

2 Draw in a small rectangle as part of the top of the lantern and draw two horizontal lines for folding later.

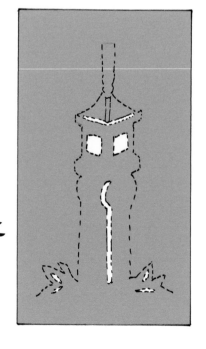

3 Cut out the design along the dotted lines as shown.

54

4 Fold up along the top horizontal line to make the base. Pull out the lantern design very gently and fold the base so that the lantern stands up.

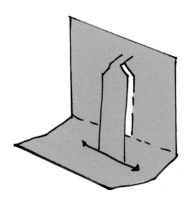

5 You can add some details with a pen.

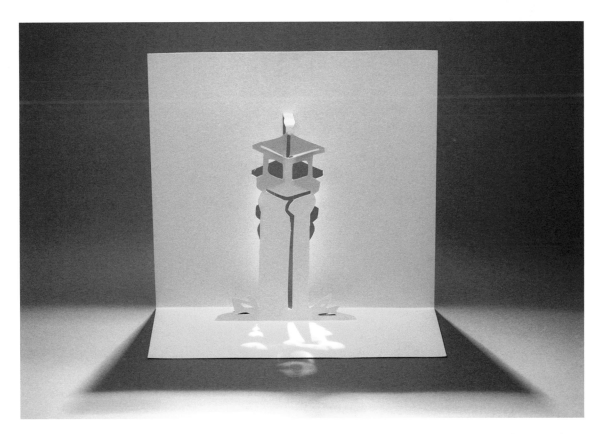

Use a small LED light to make the model really stand out.

Harp

This harp tableau shows one of my favorite musical instruments alongside other related elements such as staves and notes.

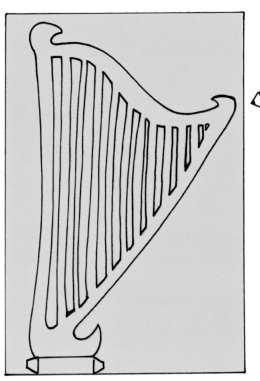

1 Using a rectangular piece of card measuring 7 x 10 cm (2¾ x 4 in), draw the design as shown.

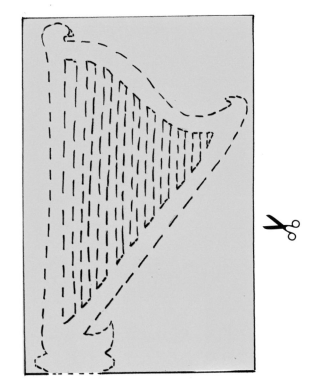

2 Cut out the harp along the dotted lines.

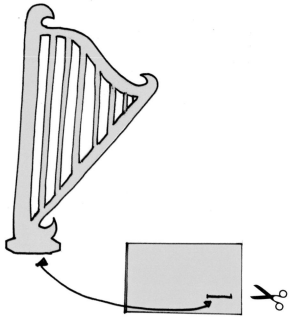

3 Take piece of rectangular card measuring 12 x 18 cm (4¾ x 7 in). This will be the base for the harp to stand on. Make a cut at the bottom right of the base to correspond with the small flap at the bottom of the harp.

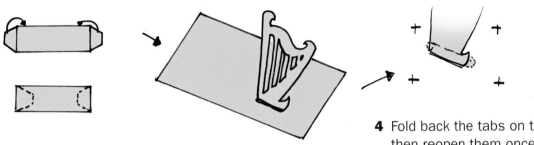

4 Fold back the tabs on the small flap, then reopen them once you have inserted the model into the base.

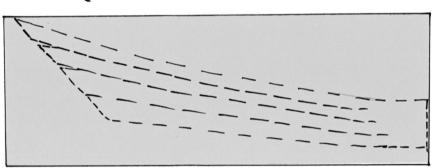

5 Using a third piece of card the same color as the harp and measuring the same as the base, draw a long shape and cut out along the dotted lines. Make sure not to cut right to the end with the internal cutting, as you want this piece to remain intact.

6 With the same color card, make another slightly different shape; it should be shorter than the first.

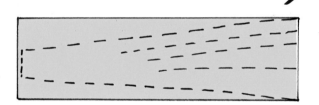

7 Cut out a few musical notes.

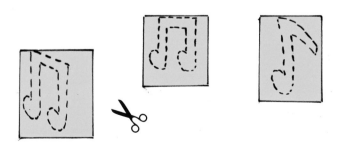

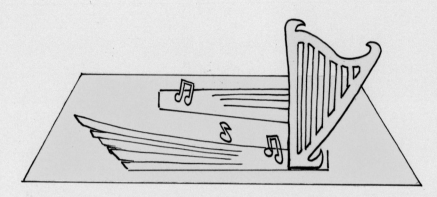

8 Now arrange all the elements as shown around the base of the harp.

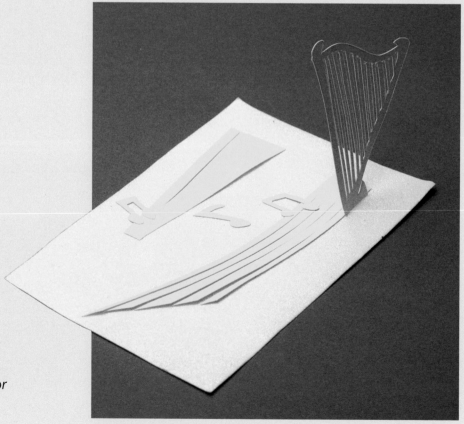

This model would make a lovely gift for a musical friend.

Lantern

Here is another version of the ever-popular Japanese lantern, using two cut-outs to create the composition.

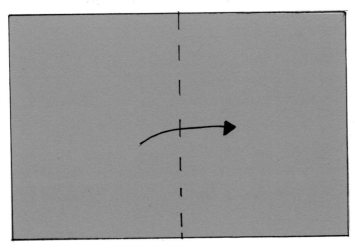

1 Fold a rectangular piece of card measuring 21 x 30 cm (8¼ x 11¾ in) in half.

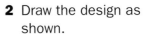

2 Draw the design as shown.

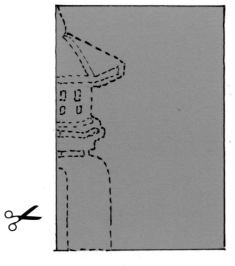

3 Cut out along the dotted lines.

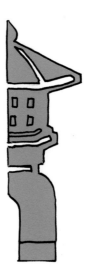

4 Open out the model.

5 Fold back the small rectangles at the base of the model so that it stands upright.

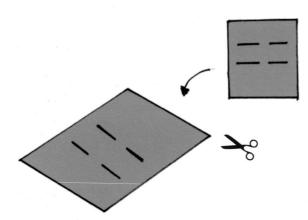

7 Take another sheet of card with the same measurements as the first. Make four short cuts to correspond with the rectangles at the base of the lanterns.

6 Now create another lantern exactly the same.

8 Insert the pagodas into the four cuts, and secure the flaps with glue.

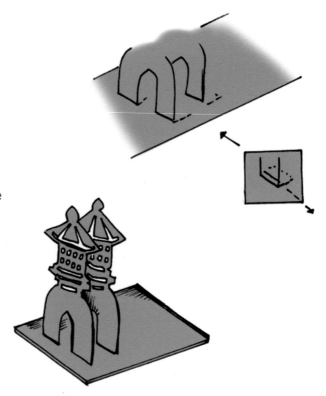

9 Attach the lanterns to the base. The model should look like this.

10 Take a sheet of card measuring 14 x 21 cm (5½ x 8¼ in) and draw on the design as shown.

11 Cut out and fold to make the surround. Place your lantern model on top.

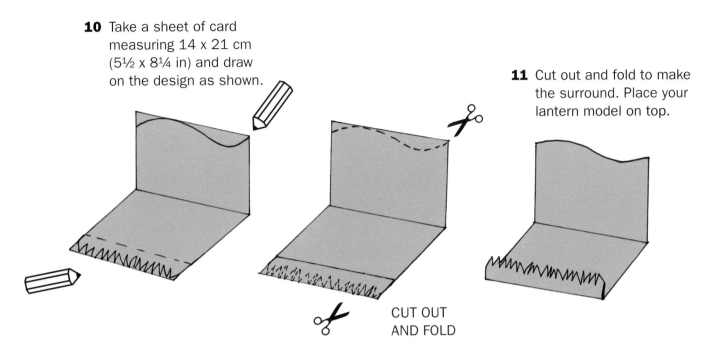

CUT OUT
AND FOLD

This model looks lovely with some LED lighting.

Mobile

Skill level | **Medium**

This geometric design gives an interesting, dynamic effect.
As it turns and moves in different directions, the cut sections
look lovely with the light shining through them.

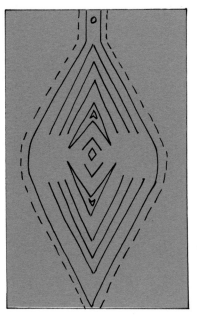

1 Take a rectangular
piece of paper
measuring
21 x 28 cm
(8¼ x 11 in), draw
the lines as shown,
then cut out the
main shape.

2 Cut carefully
along all the
dotted internal
lines.

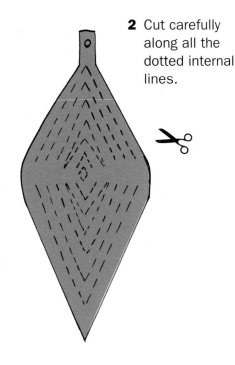

*The finished model, with
the light shining through.*

3 Fold and move the cut pieces
of paper in different directions to
create dynamism.

Cards For All Occasions

This section includes a range of greetings cards inspired by celebration, nature, and love. They all include space for writing a message; some can even be used as decorative pieces.

Butterfly

This project requires precision, but it is a beautiful and creative way to enhance a gift. It is made with colored card; you need to use a craft knife and cutting board to render the design accurately.

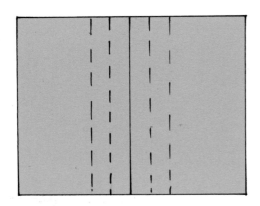

1 On a rectangular piece of colored card measuring 21 x 30 cm (8¼ x 11¾ in), draw one line down the middle and two more on either side of it at 1 cm (½ in) intervals.

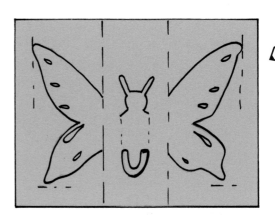

2 Draw three or four more lines, marking out the space on the card to help keep your picture balanced. Now draw your butterfly, using very light lines so that the guides won't be visible when you come to erase them.

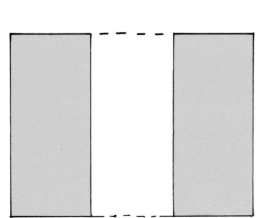

3 Using a different-colored card the same size as the first, cut out two pieces measuring 12.5 cm (5 in) across.

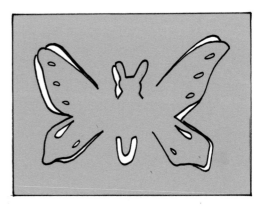

4 Using a craft knife and cutting board, cut round your design, but make sure to stop cutting the wings when you reach the lines either side of the mid-point. Cut out the head and the end of the abdomen, again avoiding the point where body and wings meet.

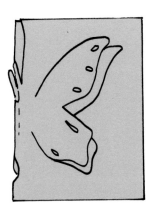

5 Fold the card in half down the middle. Then fold along the two lines either side to make an accordion pleat. Erase your guide lines.

6 Push the wings and body out and glue the pieces of card you prepared in step 3 to the back, starting from the outer edge.

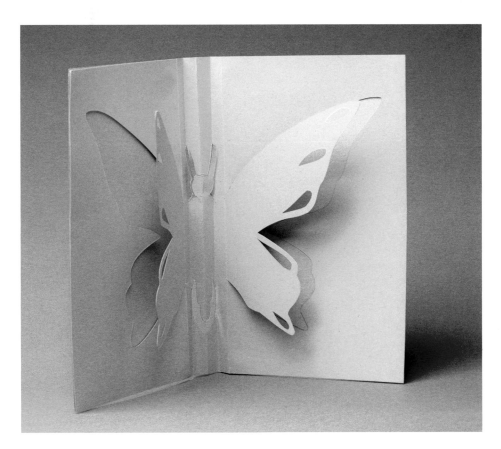

You can fold the model either way to make a card or a decorative model.

Reindeer

These two unusual Christmas cards are created with partial cutting and the shapes are pulled out to give a 3D effect.

1 Take a rectangular piece of card measuring 21 x 30 cm (8¼ x 11¾ in), fold it in half and then reopen it.

2 Draw the reindeer design as shown.

3 Cut out carefully along the dotted lines. Now glue a same-sized card of a contrasting color to the back. It's important to ensure you don't glue down any part of the cut-out.

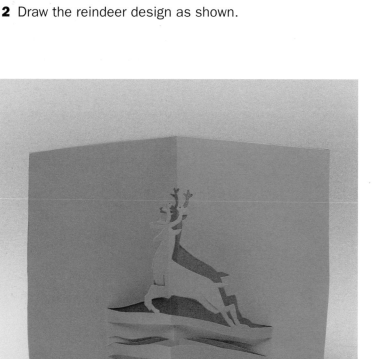

4 Gently pull forward the design so that it stands out.

Here the card is made in seasonal red and green.

Snowman

The snowman partial cut-out is in white, of course, against a colored background. With this card, you know that Christmas has truly arrived!

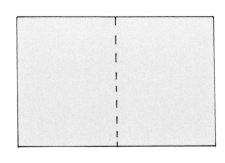

1 Take a piece of white card measuring 21 x 30 cm (8¼ x 11¾ in), fold it in half and then reopen it.

2 Draw the snowman design as shown.

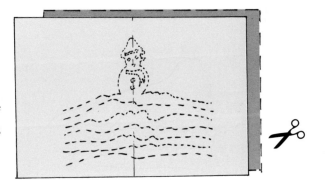

3 Cut out carefully along the dotted lines. Now glue same-sized card of a contrasting color to the back. It's important to ensure you don't glue down any part of the cut-out.

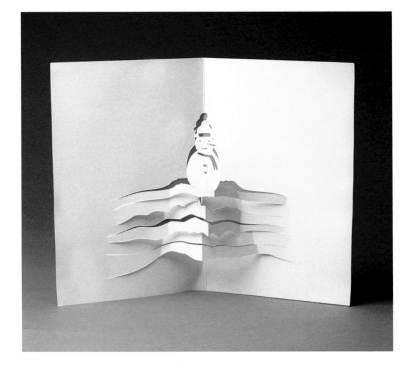

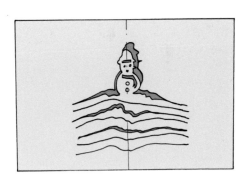

4 Gently pull forward the design so that it stands out.

You can draw on sprigs of holly and other Christmas motifs for added color.

Flower

This card has an original stylized design and uses the wraparound technique to great effect. It works best using brightly colored paper.

1 Take a rectangular piece of medium-thickness card measuring 16 x 25 cm (6¼ x 9¾ in) and fold it in half vertically to establish the mid-point. Open it and draw the design on the righthand side.

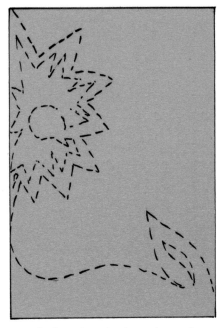

2 Cut the design along the dotted lines.

3 Make a vertical fold one-third of the way in from the left, and tuck the lefthand side under.

4 Turn the card over, open out the fold, and glue another piece of medium-thickness card to the righthand side (not the side with the flower design).

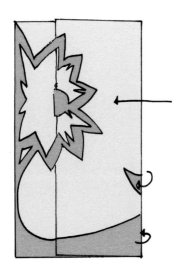

5 Fold in the righthand flap, then fold the lefthand side with the flower design over this. Fold the bottom part with the leaf around the back, folding the leaf-tip down so that it hooks over the front of the card.

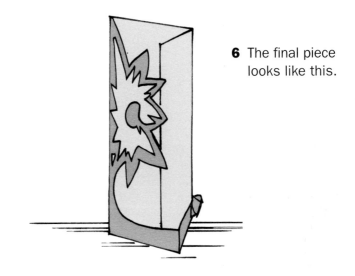

6 The final piece looks like this.

When the card is open, the leaf part stands in front.

Celebration

This project is created by making partial cuts and leaving the base attached. It works best if you use white card for the cut-out and colored card for the background.

1 Take a piece of medium-thickness card measuring 21 x 30 cm (8¼ x 11¾ in).

3 Using a craft knife and cutting board, carefully cut out along the dotted lines.

2 Draw the design as shown.

4 Fold the shape along the two dotted lines at the base and gently pull out the design.

5 Glue your design to the righthand side of a piece of card. Fold the card in half. Your final piece should look like this.

This card has been made in a reverse colorway.

Dolphins

With two dolphins leaping out of ocean waves, this design has a lovely feeling of movement and balance.

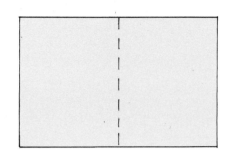

1 Take a rectangular piece of medium-thickness card measuring 21 x 30 cm (8¼ x 11¾ in) and fold to mark the mid-point.

2 Draw the design in the middle.

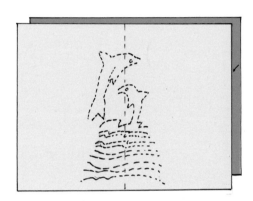

3 Using a craft knife and cutting board, carefully cut out along the dotted lines. Glue another sheet of different-colored card to the back, making sure you don't glue down the design you have just cut out.

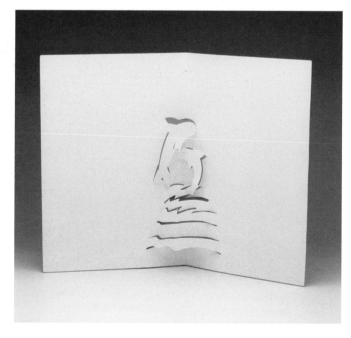

Sheets of white and blue card work well with this design.

4 Pull the design out gently for a 3D effect.

Hearts

This card has a pretty Art Nouveau-style border of hearts.
You could also use it as a photo frame.

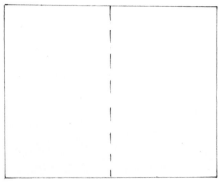

1 Take a rectangular piece of medium-thickness card measuring 21 x 30 cm (8¼ x 11¾ in), fold it to mark the mid-point, then reopen it.

2 Draw the design on the righthand side.

3 Using a craft knife and cutting board, carefully cut out along the dotted lines.

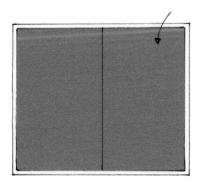

4 Glue another sheet of different-colored card to the back, making sure you don't glue down the design you have just cut out. This card can be thinner than the card you have used for the design.

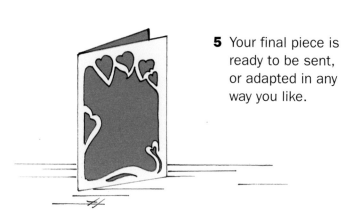

5 Your final piece is ready to be sent, or adapted in any way you like.

How about adding some glitter or dried flower petals?

Mexican eagle

This design is inspired by Aztec culture. It involves a lot of intricate cutting, so it's important to be precise with your drawing.

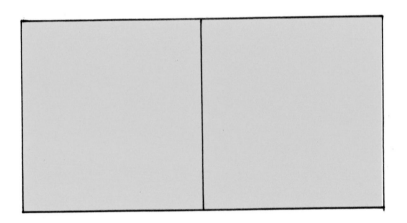

1 Take a piece of medium-thickness card measuring 15 x 30 cm (6 x 11¾ in). Fold it in half and reopen it.

2 Draw a frame with a narrow 0.5 cm (¼ in) border.

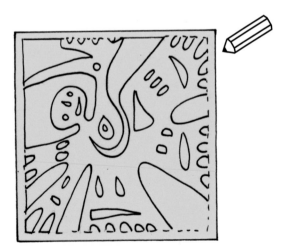

3 Now draw your design, paying attention to the details.

4 Using a craft knife and cutting board, carefully cut out along the dotted lines.

This eye-catching card is best made with brightly colored materials.

5 Glue another sheet of contrasting colored card to the back, making sure you don't glue down the design you have just cut out. This card can be thinner than the card you have used for the design.

6 Fold the card in half and admire your handiwork!

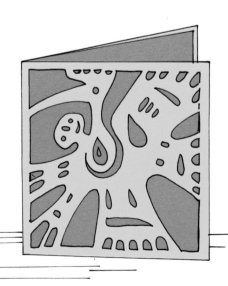

Swans

The regal swan makes a perfect focus for this pretty card.

2 Cut out along the dotted lines.

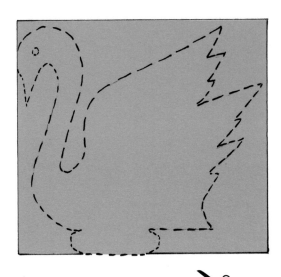

1 Take a sheet of fairly thick card measuring 15 x 30 cm (6 x 11¾ in) and fold it in half vertically. Draw the design as shown.

2b Your cut-out will look like this.

3 Open it to see the design as a mirror shape.

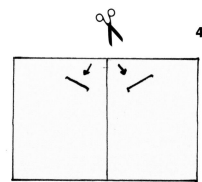

4 & 5 Take a sheet of a different-colored/patterned card measuring 6 x 12 cm (2½ x 4¾ in) and make two cuts as shown. These should be the same length as the swan bases minus the flaps on either side.

6 Fold back the small lateral triangles on the swan bases, then insert them through the cuts you have just made.

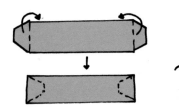

7 This is how they look on the back of the card. Now reopen the triangles.

Swans continued

8 Draw three hearts on the base card and cut them out along the dotted lines.

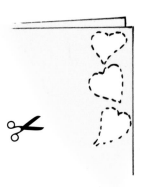

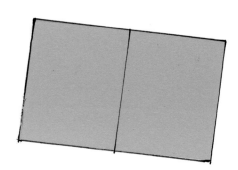

9 You could glue a piece of colored card to the back of the model, so that it is visible through the hearts. This model can be left flat as a decoration (see left).

10 Or it can be used closed, like this, as a greetings card.

Patterned card makes an effective background.

Landscape

This card is inspired by nature and the countryside. It has some intricate cutting and looks great if you use another card or paper of a different color inside.

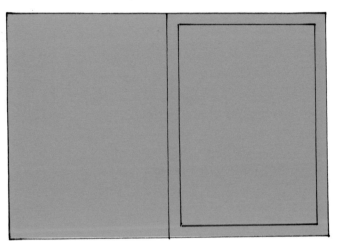

1 Take a sheet of card measuring 21 x 30 cm (8¼ x 11¾ in) and fold it in half vertically. Draw a frame with a border of about 0.5cm (¼ in) on the righthand side, as shown.

2 Draw your design and cut it out along the dotted lines.

3 Fold the card in half.

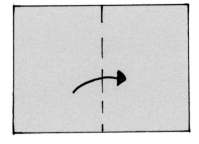

4 Take a sheet of paper the same size but of a different color, fold it in half and glue down the righthand side, making sure you don't glue down the design you have just cut out.

5 The final piece should look like this.

Different shades of green work well for this peaceful scene.

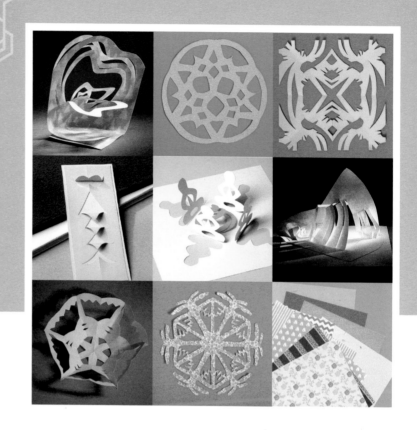

Modern and Abstract

These projects are inspired by modern forms and take kirigami to an interesting new level. You will find some intriguing abstract sculptures here as well as practical modern designs.

Abstract 1

This piece is inspired by sculptural forms and movement. It is created by simple but precise cutting and looks great in a pale color with some moody low lighting.

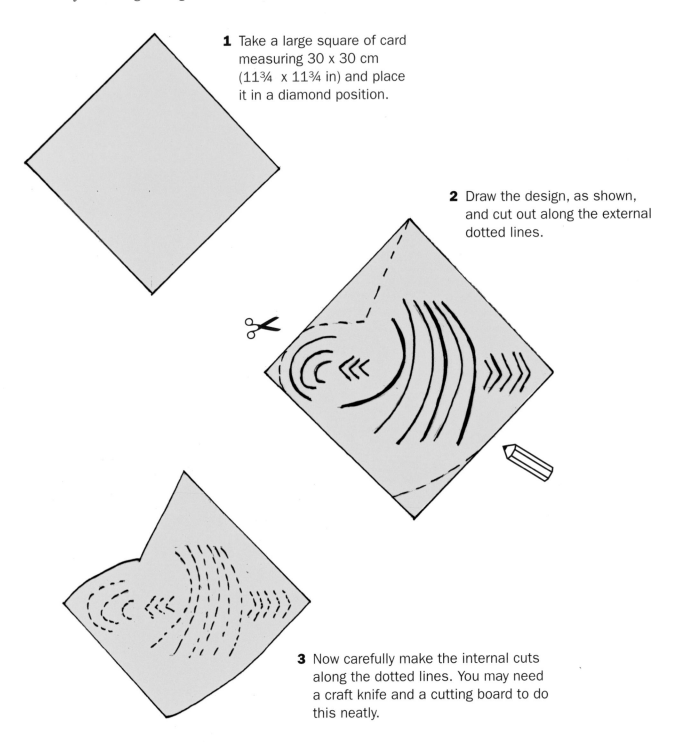

1 Take a large square of card measuring 30 x 30 cm (11¾ x 11¾ in) and place it in a diamond position.

2 Draw the design, as shown, and cut out along the external dotted lines.

3 Now carefully make the internal cuts along the dotted lines. You may need a craft knife and a cutting board to do this neatly.

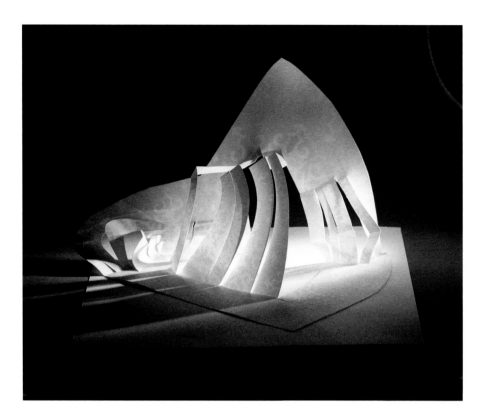

Illuminate the model from inside for a dramatic effect.

4 Pull out all the pieces of your cut-out, creating folds at various angles (nearly 90° for the middle section).

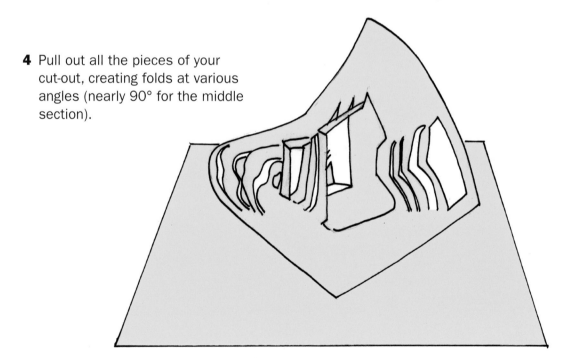

5 Glue the lower two sides of your diamond shape to another square of card, but don't attach the lefthand tip.

Abstract 2

This piece is inspired by modern building forms. It works well when attached to a rigid base like an architectural model.

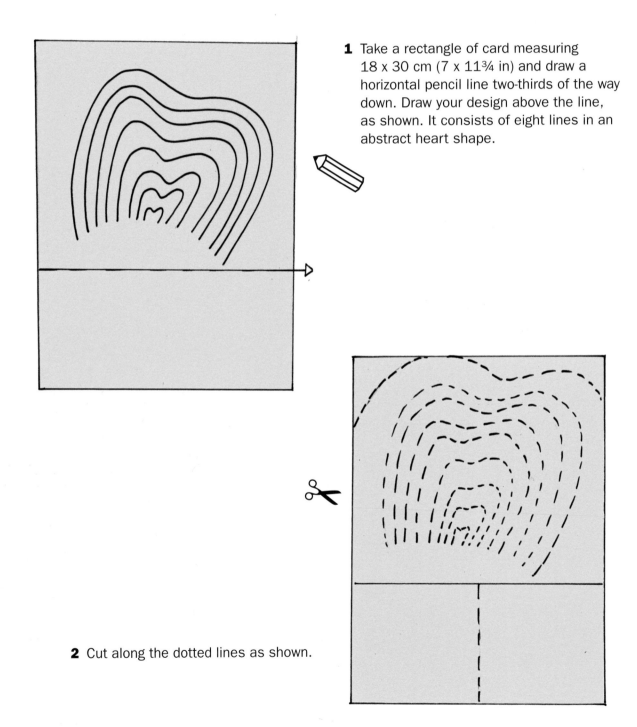

1 Take a rectangle of card measuring 18 x 30 cm (7 x 11¾ in) and draw a horizontal pencil line two-thirds of the way down. Draw your design above the line, as shown. It consists of eight lines in an abstract heart shape.

2 Cut along the dotted lines as shown.

3 Pull the lefthand flap over the right, folding slightly as you go.

5 Move the cut-out elements around until you have a pleasing shape.

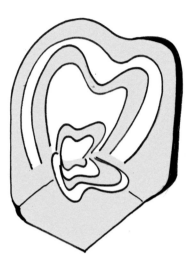

4 Align the edges and glue the flaps together.

Soft lighting works well with this model.

Celtic coaster

This coaster is inspired by Irish culture and designs. The simple shape looks lovely made with sparkling paper and used as a coaster.

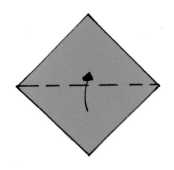

1 Take a square of paper or card measuring 14 x 14 cm (5½ x 5½ in) and fold it in half upward on the diagonal.

2 Measure a 60° angle from the mid-point.

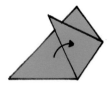

3 Fold in the righthand side.

4 Fold the lefthand side on top.

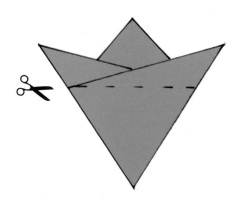

5 Cut along the line.

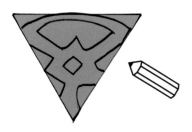

6 Draw the design as shown.

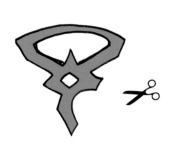

7 Cut it out and
open out the paper.

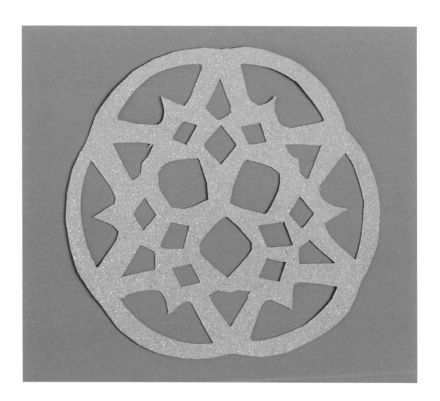

Gold and green is the ideal color combination for this piece.

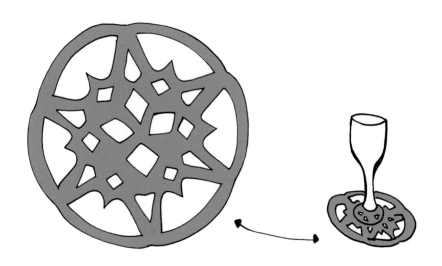

Abstract bowl

The cuts in this project are abstract and geometric, but the final effect is a decorative bowl that makes a lovely ornament.

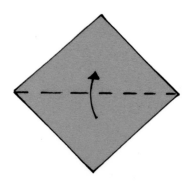

2 Measure a 60° angle from the mid-point.

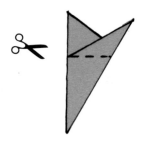

3 Fold in the righthand side.

1 Take a square of medium-thickness card measuring 22 x 22 cm (8½ x 8½ in) and fold it in half on the diagonal.

4 Fold the lefthand side on top, then fold the model in half again.

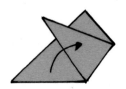

5 Cut along the line.

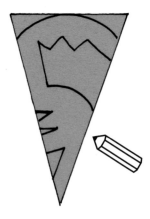

6 Draw the design as shown.

7 Cut it out and open out the paper.

9 Pinch and glue these folds together.

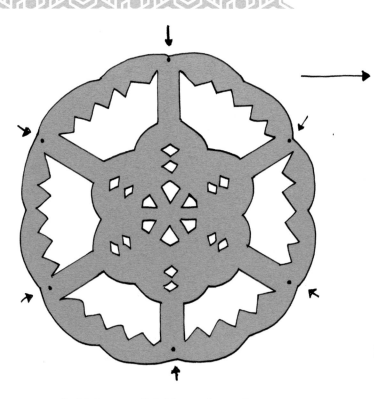

8 Make small folds at the points shown here with dots.

10 As you are gluing the folds, push the shape towards the middle and flatten down the base as much as possible.

11 The final piece should look like this.

Made with brightly colored card, the bowl is an attractive decorative piece.

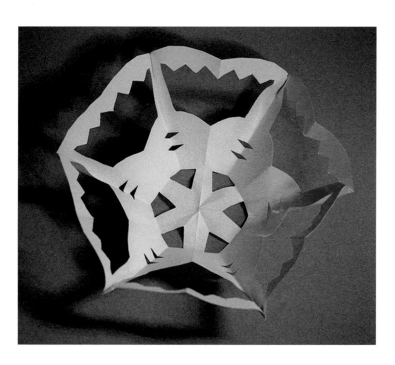

Bookmark

This design is inspired by the Easter Island statues.

1 Draw the design on a piece of card measuring 5 x 15 cm (2 x 6 in).

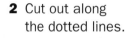

2 Cut out along the dotted lines.

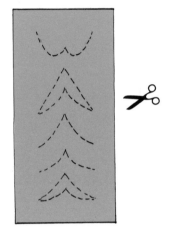

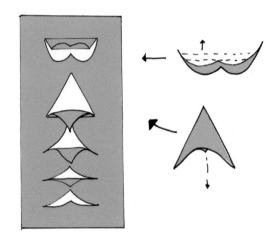

3 Fold the cuttings as shown.

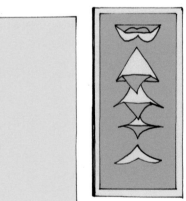

4 Take a piece of slightly larger card in a contrasting color and glue it to the back of your design.

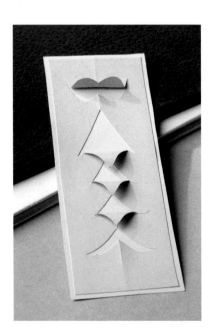

The bookmark is both pretty and useful.

5 The final piece is now ready to use.

Cutout

This design looks lovely created in bright colors.

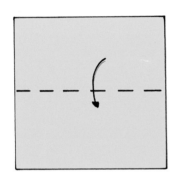

1 Take a square of medium-thickness card measuring 21 x 21 cm (8¼ x 8¼ in) and fold it in half downward.

2 Fold it in half again, from left to right.

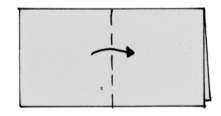

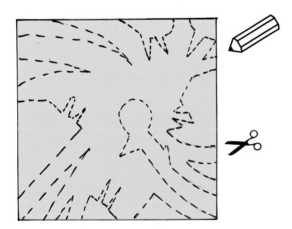

3 Draw the design on the square you have made, then cut along the dotted lines.

4 Open out the paper to reveal the final design.

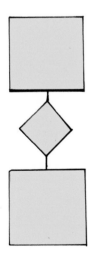

5 You can use this on its own as a decorative piece or make two larger pieces and hang all three together as a triptych.

This vibrant design can be adapted for various uses.

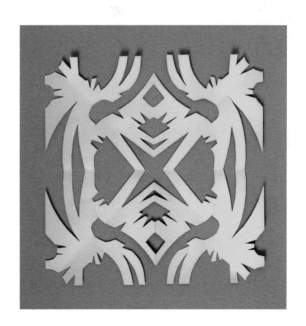

Meditation

Another inspirational project inspired by shapes reminiscent of Buddhism or yoga, this design can be used as a calming table decoration.

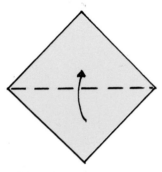

1 Take a square of paper or thin card measuring 21 x 21 cm (8¼ x 8¼ in) and fold it in half upward on the diagonal.

2 Fold it in half again from left to right.

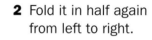

3 This is your base.

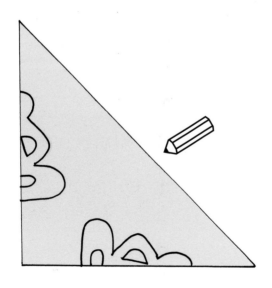

4 Draw the design as shown.

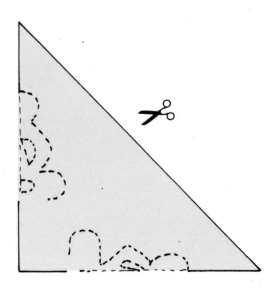

5 Cut along the dotted lines only.

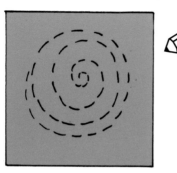

7 Cut out the shape along the dotted lines and pull up the spiral.

6 Using another piece of paper of a different color, draw a spiral shape.

8 Place this spiral in the middle of your design.

Pull up the four figures in your model so that they are sitting in a meditative pose.

Mandala

The final project is inspired by the Asian tradition of the mandala, which symbolizes the universe and life.

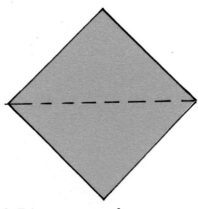

1 Take a square of paper or card measuring 21 x 21 cm (8¼ x 8¼ in) and fold it in half upward on the diagonal.

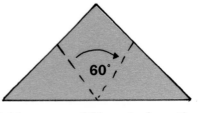

2 Measure a 60° angle from the mid-point.

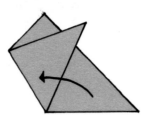

3 Fold in the lefthand side.

4 Fold the righthand side on top.

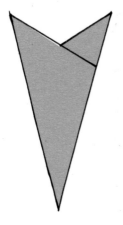

5 Fold in half from left to right.

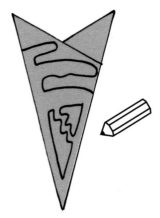

6 Draw the design as shown.

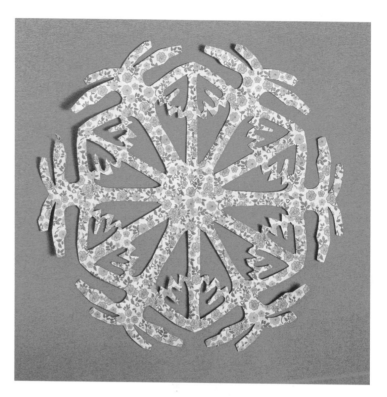

This elegant mandala can be made in plain or patterned paper.

7 Cut it out along the lines and open out the paper.

8 The final piece should look like this.

Stockists

The following suppliers stock a wide range of materials for kirigami enthusiasts:

www.aliexpress.com/w/wholesale-origami-paper.html
www.foldedsquare.com
www. japancentre.com/en/categories/1057-origami
www.origami.com.au
www.origami-fun.com
www.origamipapermonster.com
www.theorigamipapershop.com
www.origamishop.us
www.paperchase.co.uk
www.roze.co.uk/origami-paper-22-c.asp
supplies.britishorigami.info
www.thejapaneseshop.co.uk

All illustrations and models by Monika Cilmi
Photos by Will White